DISCOVERING TURNER

ROBERT CUMMING

DISCOVERING TURNER

TATE GALLERY

cover
The Shipwreck (detail)

ISBN 1 85437 039 1
Published by order of the Trustees 1990
Designed by Caroline Johnston
Published by Tate Gallery Publications, Millbank, London SW1P 4RG
Copyright © 1990 The Tate Gallery All rights reserved

Printed on Parilux matt 150gsm and typeset in Baskerville
Printed by Balding + Mansell Limited, Wisbech, Cambs

The publication of this book has been made possible
by generous support from British Gas plc

British Gas

Contents

Introduction [7]

1 The Shipwreck [9]

2 Snow Storm: Hannibal and his Army
Crossing the Alps [12]

3 The Decline of the Carthaginian Empire [16]

4 England: Richmond Hill, on the Prince
Regent's Birthday [20]

5 The Golden Bough [24]

6 Petworth Park, Tillington Church in the Distance [28]

7 Bridge of Sighs, Ducal Palace and Custom-House
Venice: Canaletti Painting [32]

8 Norham Castle, Sunrise [36]

9 Peace – Burial at Sea [42]

10 Snow Storm – Steamboat off a Harbour's Mouth [46]

Turner [51]

Turner's Times [62]

The Clore Gallery for the Turner Collection, London

Introduction

There are many ways of looking at pictures and enjoying them. There can be things to recognise, stories to learn or remember, secret and hidden meanings to unravel, dreams and fantasies to explore and share. As well as painting glorious pictures, Turner loved to look at the work of other artists, and he was always willing to travel long distances to see paintings at first hand, with his own eyes. Because Turner was a painter he also knew it was important to look at the way paintings are made – their size and shape, the texture of paint, forms and patterns and actual colours, – for they are things which we ought to notice and experience if we are to appreciate and understand pictures fully.

Turner's works are shown in a new and separate building at the Tate Gallery in London. It is called the Clore Gallery, named after the family who gave the money for the building. It is very rare for an artist to have his own gallery, and this honour is a mark of Turner's importance and achievement. In the first part of this book I have chosen a number of paintings from the Turner Collection in the Clore and looked at them in detail. Then, in the second part, I have discussed the sort of person Turner was and the age he lived in. I have no doubt that he is one of the greatest painters of all time. He also lived through a very exciting period of history.

If you have not seen Turner's work before I hope this book will encourage you to go and have a look at his paintings for yourself. Seeing Turner's pictures for the first time will be an exciting experience, full of surprises, and may be the start of a lifetime's friendship with this great artist. If you do know Turner's pictures already, I hope this book will help you to take your friendship further.

Robert Cumming

[1]

The Shipwreck
1805

Can you see where the shipwreck is?
Most people take some time to discover it.
Follow the small boats which are rescuing the sailors and passengers and you will find it – a large sailing ship which is half-hidden by the large bright sail in the centre. Even the rescuing boats are in trouble. The one on the left is about to go down, and another in the centre is about to be swamped by a large wave. It looks as though the efforts of the sailors in the boat on the right will be in vain.

Turner made many sea voyages. He went by boat to the Hebrides off the north-west coast of Scotland. He crossed the Channel to France several times. When he first sailed to Calais in 1802 it was stormy and he was nearly thrown into the sea. However, as I am sure you can tell from this picture, Turner loved danger. In fact the very first painting that Turner showed at the annual exhibition at the Royal Academy of Arts in London was about danger at sea. It is 'Fishermen at Sea', and you can see it near 'The Shipwreck'.

Turner enjoyed storms at sea because they demonstrated how mighty and powerful the forces of nature can be, and how small and feeble human beings are by comparison. This celebration of the power and force of nature is the theme of many of Turner's paintings.

How does Turner put such a strong sense of movement and force and danger into his picture? There are the small boats being tossed by the huge waves and the activity of the people in them with their desperate faces. The boats and the waves are arranged in an enormous circle like a

whirlpool, or vortex. Turner makes his white and green paint for the sea rough in texture like the foaming of rough water. And, apart from the large light-coloured sail which stands out strongly and seems ready to crash into the middle of the whirlpool, he uses dark, angry colours.

[2]

Snow Storm: Hannibal and his Army Crossing the Alps
1812

Before I tell you about Hannibal, have a good look to see what is in the picture. Can you see the elephant with its rider and waving trunk? It is silhouetted against the bright sky to the left of centre of this painting. In the foreground are sharp rocks and groups of soldiers who are crouching and raising their arms. Most of the painting is taken up by a swirling snow storm which is sweeping down the mountains. It is pitch-black on the right, but on the left the sun is trying to shine through, and in the top left-hand corner you can see a patch of blue sky.

Hannibal was the leader of the Carthaginians, a powerful nation who lived in North Africa about 2,000 years ago. Their land is now called Tunisia. They were the main rivals of the Roman Empire and in 218 BC they attempted to invade Italy and defeat the Romans. Hannibal equipped a huge army and used elephants for transport. He marched his army from North Africa to Spain, then to France. Eventually he tried to cross the Alps to march south into Italy. However, the cold and the storms and the hardship of the mountains were too much for his men (and the elephants) and when they reached Italy they were so weakened that they were unable to march on Rome to capture it as they had planned.

This painting is in many ways very typical of Turner. There is the subject of the destructive powers of nature, and the swirling, vortex-like composition that we saw in 'The Shipwreck'. The painting is also very topical, for Turner had seen the rise of a great empire in his lifetime and was beginning to see its fall. This was the French empire of Napoleon, and

1812, the year in which this picture was exhibited at the Royal Academy, was the year of Napoleon's first major setback, his retreat from Moscow (which Tchaikovsky later celebrated in his famous 1812 Overture). Like Hannibal, Napoleon was also defeated by the cruel, destructive forces of nature, in his case the Russian winter.

There is also a true story which tells how this picture was first inspired by a real storm. In 1810 Turner was staying with friends in Yorkshire. Whilst walking on the Yorkshire Moors with a young companion called Hawkesworth Fawkes he saw a storm in the distance. Hawkesworth later explained what happened: '. . . he [Turner] was making notes of its form and colour on the back of a letter . . . He was absorbed, he was entranced. There was the storm rolling and sweeping and shafting out its lightning over the Yorkshire hills. Presently the storm passed, and he finished. "There," said he, "Hawkey, in two years you will see this again, and call it Hannibal Crossing the Alps."' It is a good story which shows how Turner used his powerful imagination: he could see one thing, but already his mind was transforming it into another idea and message.

[3]

The Decline of the Carthaginian Empire
1817

The first thing I always notice in this picture is the sun. Turner has put it at the very centre, a thick round disc of yellow paint. So I think we should ask: Why has Turner made the sun so important? Turner is using the sun as a symbol. While the sun sets so does the might of the Carthaginian Empire (which we talked about in *Illustration 2*) and it is not difficult to see why. In the foreground are musical instruments, flowers, and bottles of wine. The people are richly dressed and are mainly interested in enjoying themselves. Only the woman sitting on the wall on the right seems to be unhappy. In other words Turner is using the light and the subject of the painting to spell out a moral: nations which lose themselves in pleasure will die. His full title for the picture is 'The Decline of the Carthaginian Empire – Rome being determined on the Overthrow of her Hated Rival, demanded from her such Terms as might force her into War, or ruin her by Compliance: the Enervated [i.e. weak and lazy] Carthaginians, in their Anxiety for Peace, consented to give up their Arms and their Children.' Turner sometimes used long titles like this to explain the meaning of his pictures, and perhaps to make us look more closely at them.

This is an imaginary view of Carthage, of course, but it shows us again what a powerful and inventive imagination Turner had. It is also important to realise that Turner painted another similar picture which was called 'Dido Building Carthage'. Dido was queen of Tyre. After the murder of her husband, the king, she fled to North Africa. There she founded the city of Carthage. As you might guess, Turner showed a sunrise to symbolise the founding of the Empire. This painting hangs in the National Gallery in Trafalgar Square with a selection of other

masterpieces by him. When he died Turner left 'Dido Building Carthage' and another painting to the National Gallery with the demand that they should always be on show, and always hang next to two pictures by Turner's artistic hero, the great seventeenth-century French artist Claude Lorraine. Claude also painted works with a framework of buildings and figures, with the view directly into the sun in the centre. Turner admired these paintings enormously, and like all creative painters he was never too proud to learn from the success of others. He would often borrow (but not slavishly copy) ideas which he then developed into his own style of painting. So the sun is important for a second reason: Turner is asking us to recognise the influence on him of the great old master painter, Claude.

This is a large painting and it was intended to make a sensation at the Royal Academy's annual exhibition where it would have been in competition with a vast number of other works. Turner was ambitious: he liked to be noticed and he liked to be thought the best. The critics praised the picture highly, and everyone would have been conscious that only two years before this picture was exhibited Wellington had finally defeated Napoleon and the French Empire at Waterloo.

While you are in this room, have a look at 'Crossing the Brook'. This is another picture where Turner has borrowed ideas from Claude. It is a view of the Tamar Valley in Devon, but he has deliberately turned it into a view which looks like Italy, and very much like an old master painting.

[4]

England: Richmond Hill, on the Prince Regent's Birthday

1819

In this picture Turner gives us a typical English scene. It is a view from Richmond Hill near London and it is very much the same today. The river is the Thames and as a boy Turner was brought up near it in Covent Garden in the centre of London. Throughout his life he loved the river, and when he became successful he bought a house near Richmond, within the view shown here. In the foreground a large group of people can be seen enjoying the summer weather; there are children with their toys, soldiers, pretty girls, and dogs chasing about. Nearer to us there are musical instruments and there is a flag caught up in the tree to the right of centre. To the left and beside the river are some tiny figures in white playing cricket. On the river is a barge which you can see has brightly coloured decorations. The Prince Regent, who later became George IV, had visited Richmond Hill on 10 August 1818, his birthday, and this is probably the barge he used.

This is one of Turner's largest paintings, and it demonstrates his skill in creating a sense of space and light. Notice how he does this: he makes you turn your head to the left to look past the two trees to the cricket match and on into the far distance. Then he makes your head turn again across the centre of the painting to the right where you look down the path to a group of figures near a clump of trees. There is a clear open sky and the top branches and leaves on the trees seem to be caught by a gentle breeze. Turner builds up this feeling of light and air and space by placing the foreground in shadow, so that it makes a contrast with the light by the

river in the distance. But this foreground shadow is also pierced by flashes of bright light.

I think that in this picture Turner is indicating his pride in being an Englishman. As he had just lived through a major war when the English way of life was threatened, his feelings are understandable. There are other paintings in this room which also refer to the English way of life and which show how well Turner could capture the cool silvery and soft light of the English countryside. They are:

Ploughing up Turnips near Slough. Windsor Castle in the background.

London from Greenwich. Greenwich Hospital, the home of the Royal Naval College, is in the middle distance.

Frosty Morning. One of Turner's favourite pictures which captures the atmosphere of a cold winter day.

[5]

The Golden Bough
1834

What impresses me first about the picture is the glow of warm light and colour. It seems to shine out of the painting, and is very different from the dark colours that Turner used in 'The Shipwreck' (*Illustration 1*) or 'Hannibal Crossing the Alps' (*Illustration 2*). In the foreground are some tiny figures and animals. The girl on the left is holding a garland or bough over her head. On the right by the ruins you can see a snake and a fox. The lake and the hills in the distance become lost in the shimmering haze that we occasionally see on summer days in England, but more often in the countries of Southern Europe.

This is another painting where Turner has remembered what he has seen, but used his own imagination and his readings from books to invent a wonderful picture. In 1819 he went to Italy for the first time and experienced the warm golden light there, which is quite different from the cool grey light of Northern Europe. He made a second visit in 1829, and he has used his observations and memory of Italian light and landscape to create the space and glow in this painting. His visits to Italy were very important to his development as a painter. As well as discovering a new kind of light, he was also visiting the birthplace of some of the greatest painters in history, such as Raphael, Titian and Leonardo da Vinci. At the same time he was seeing at first hand the land of the Roman Empire, and we have already noticed Turner's fascination with ancient history.

Turner's interest in Italian light is easy for us to follow because we can see it with our own eyes. It is not easy for us to follow his reference to the Golden Bough of the picture title because we rarely read the books which were familiar to Turner and all well-educated people in the early

nineteenth century. The picture takes us back to ancient Italy. There was a Prince of Troy called Aeneas who escaped with a group of companions after the Greeks sacked his city. They sailed to Italy where they consulted an oracle, or fortune teller. Aeneas asked if he could see his dead father once more. The oracle, who had the power to grant the wish, agreed. Aeneas had to descend to the underworld, which was inhabited by the dead, holding a branch or bough of mistletoe to protect himself. In this picture we cannot see Aeneas, but the girl holding the bough, which she has just cut with her sickle, is the oracle. She is waiting for the arrival of Aeneas.

In the underworld Aeneas met his father who showed him the souls of his descendants who were not yet born, predicting that they would become kings and emperors of Rome. Aeneas and his companions were the legendary ancestors of the Roman people. The book which Turner had read was the *Aeneid*, by the Roman author Virgil. So in several different ways Turner's picture is about Italy: the light, the ancient history, the writers, and the painters he so admired and borrowed from.

There is an amusing story about the way this picture was finished. Turner had all but completed it, and decided to add a nude figure in the foreground. He went to the life class at the Royal Academy one evening and made a sketch in his notebook. The next day he found it was exactly the right size, so he cut out the paper and stuck it on to the painting, intending to paint it properly later. He forgot. After he had sold the picture the paper started to peel off, and when this was pointed out to Turner he went to the owner and painted in the group of three figures which you can see in the centre.

[6]

Petworth Park, Tillington Church in the Distance
*c.*1828

I have chosen this painting for several reasons. It is painted in a very free and sketchy way, and it is small in size. There is not much detail to see, and nothing that is difficult to understand. We look westward across the park of a grand house towards the setting sun. In the distance the church tower is silhouetted against the sky. The figure walking towards the house is George Wyndham, third Earl of Egremont, the owner of the house and a friend of Turner's. His dogs are rushing from the house to greet him.

The house is Petworth House in Sussex. It is now owned by the National Trust, which looks after buildings and land that form part of our national heritage, and it is open to the public. You can still see the view of the park in this picture from the dining room window. It has changed very little since Turner's day, although at one time there was a proposal to put a motorway through it! It is very likely that Turner sat at the dining room window to paint this sketch: we can tell it was painted rapidly from the loose, rough way he applied the paint. He also made a number of pencil studies of this view, and from the oil sketch and the pencil studies he painted a detailed and finished painting which now hangs in the dining-room at Petworth, opposite the very window where he would have sat with his easel. Artists often work in this way – painting quick sketches at the scene, and then using these to work from in their studio to produce a larger finished picture. The long shape of the picture was necessary as the finished work was designed to fit into a space in the old panelling of the dining-room. There were four such spaces, and in this gallery you can see other sketches which Turner made. They are

The Lake, from Petworth House, Sunset
Chichester Canal
The Chain Pier, Brighton
A Ship Aground

Turner did not use this last sketch, but the others were worked up into the finished pictures which are still at Petworth.

  I think this painting of Petworth also helps us to realise how much preliminary work goes into a finished painting – which may be the only one we see. It also shows Turner in a homely light, taking pleasure in a wonderful view and sunset. Turner never married and had no conventional family life, but although he was shy he liked the company of kindred spirits, and especially enjoyed entertaining children. He spent a lot of time at Petworth in the 1820s and 1830s relaxing in the company of George Wyndham's family and the atmosphere of the house, and studying the Petworth collection of old master paintings. He had a studio there, and many of the works he painted were made for his own pleasure rather than to impress the critics or make a splash in public. There is a very private side to Turner's character which we can begin to understand from the paintings in this gallery.

[7]

Bridge of Sighs, Ducal Palace and Custom-House, Venice: Canaletti Painting
1833

In this painting we follow Turner back to Italy. This time he is in Venice and he has chosen one of the most famous views in the world. The large pink building in the middle is the Palace of the Dukes, or Doges, of Venice, and behind it you can see two white domes of St Mark's Cathedral. The Bridge of Sighs connects the Doges' Palace with the low white building to the right, which is the prison. Trials took place in the Doges' Palace and one can imagine the sighs of the prisoners as they crossed the bridge which gave them their last sight of freedom before they were locked away; and that is how the bridge got its name. The custom house is the building on the left. In its heyday Venice had been a great trading empire, like the British Empire in Turner's day, and with his love of history Turner was well aware of the similarities between the two nations. In the left foreground you can make out a figure painting at an easel. Canaletto is shown painting away at a framed canvas. This was perhaps included as a joke, as Turner would have known perfectly well that Canaletto would have painted such finished pictures back in the studio. Canaletto, one of the most celebrated painters of picturesque views in the eighteenth century, was a Venetian and he was especially famous for his views of the canals in Venice, from which he got his name.

Turner visited Venice on two or three occasions and obviously enjoyed his visits. As well as all its historical connections, Venice has a magical atmosphere created by the effects of light and water, and this would have delighted Turner. He stayed at the Europa Hotel which overlooks the

Grand Canal. (It is just out of view to the left of this painting.) Paintings like this one were made in Turner's studio in London. In Venice, as on all his travels, Turner made pencil sketches by day in small notebooks. At night in the hotel he would make rapid sketches in watercolour, from memory. He would later use both types of sketch to make the oil paintings on his return home. His amazing visual memory enabled him to recall the atmosphere, colour and detail of a place long after he had left it.

The framed paintings in this room are finished works which Turner would have exhibited. The unframed works are sketches or experiments which were found in his studio when he died.

This painting is quite small and was intended to appeal to private collectors. It was bought by Robert Vernon, a businessman who made a fortune providing horses for the British Army during the Napoleonic Wars. He gave his collection of pictures to the nation, and you can still see his name prominently on the frame.

[8]

Norham Castle, Sunrise *c*.1845

8A Scarborough *c*.1825

8B Petworth: The Old Library. 'The Artist and his Admirers' *c*.1827

8C Valley of Splügen 1843

I have chosen three watercolours and one oil painting because there are several things that I would like to show you.

In oil paintings the colours, or pigments as they are technically called, are mixed with turpentine or oil, and they are painted onto canvas or wood. Turner nearly always used canvas, although *Illustration 7* is, in fact, painted onto a wooden panel. Oil paints have a number of important qualities. They can be used thickly or thinly depending on how they are mixed, and they can be used thickly and thinly in the same picture. They are very suitable for large size pictures, and they are comparatively strong and can be exposed to light without serious fading or harm.

In watercolours the pigments are mixed with water, and they are painted onto paper. Watercolour paints are fragile, and fade quickly in strong light (ultra violet light is the real danger). They are sometimes mixed and applied opaquely (the correct technical term for this is 'gouache'), but often they are applied in thin transparent washes which can create beautiful effects.

The Clore Gallery exhibits watercolours in a special room with dim lights to protect them, and they change them regularly to avoid too long an exposure to light. If a watercolour you want to see is not on show you can apply to look at it in the Study Room.

Turner painted literally thousands of watercolours, so it has been difficult to select only three. I have chosen 'Scarborough' because it is painted with a lot of detail, and it is full of light and colour. He intended his watercolours of this kind to be exhibited and sold, and in many cases skilled engravers made copies of them on steel and copper plates for printing book illustrations. 'Petworth: The Old Library' is a quick sketch on coloured paper. He has used both opaque gouache and transparent watercolour paint. It was made for Turner's own pleasure or for his friends, and not for exhibition. 'Valley of Splügen' has washes of thin paint over which Turner has drawn details in red ink. It is a page from a sketchbook which Turner used on a visit probably during the summer of 1841, and it is one of the many that Turner made of the Rhine Valley in Germany and Switzerland – this, too, was a sketch that Turner did for himself, without intending to exhibit it.

The oil painting I have chosen is 'Norham Castle, Sunrise', because it shows Turner experimenting with paints and colour. Turner has used oil paints, but he has diluted them so that they have become thin and transparent – in fact they appear rather like the watercolours we have looked at, especially 'Valley of Splügen'. Turner was an enormously gifted watercolour painter, and I feel sure that he has been experimenting here with oil paints to see if he could get the same luminous effect. Also, he has turned the scene into a wonderful glow of delicate pure colours, so that we think more of light itself than the castle at the centre. One thing I would like you to notice about his use of colour is the way he creates the sensation of warmth and coolness. A central patch of cool blue and cool yellow is contrasted with the small but essential accent of warm red in the cow in the foreground. If you take away the warm red the coolness of the blue and yellow are lost.

'Norham Castle, Sunrise' is also unfinished, so we can be sure that Turner did not intend it to be exhibited. In his day people would have found it difficult to appreciate its beauty because they liked paintings with

8a

8b

8c

a high degree of finish, in which they could see the amount of detailed work that the artist had put into the picture. But our eyes are familiar with modern styles in which finish is no longer considered important. So we can appreciate Turner's picture quite easily.

The subject of the painting is Norham Castle which is on the English–Scottish border, and overlooks the River Tweed near Berwick. It was already a ruin in Turner's day. He must have been particularly fascinated by its beauty and history for he painted it many times, first in *c.* 1798 when he was about 23, and throughout his life when he was travelling to Scotland or the North.

[9]

Peace – Burial at Sea
1842

At the centre of this painting is a paddle-steamer. Its chimney belches out black smoke against the evening sky, and its sails are a black silhouette. They throw black reflections on the sea, and if you look carefully you will see the flag of the ship is at half-mast. We can interpret the evening sky, the black sails, the flag and the smoke as symbols of death, and this is the subject of the picture.

It commemorates a real event. Turner's friend and rival, Sir David Wilkie, the most celebrated Scottish painter of the day, had died on board ship on his way home from a painting expedition in Egypt. He was buried at sea, off Gibraltar – you can see the famous rock in the distance – and the glow behind the paddle of the ship is the light of torches held by the ship's crew as they lower the coffin into the sea. Turner has therefore recorded what is perhaps the most moving moment in any burial service, the moment when the coffin carrying the body is finally laid to rest.

Let me pick out what the painting can tell us about Turner. In the foreground a bird is skimming across the surface of the sea. It is a duck – perhaps a mallard – and very much alive. Turner's middle name was Mallord, and he was known to joke about its similarity to mallard, and he often introduced harmless jokes and puns like this into his pictures. Turner was also very competitive and did not like to be outdone by other artists. Sir David Wilkie was famous for the skilful way he used black paint, and Turner seems to be trying to have the last word – to show that he could use black even more effectively than his friend.

Notice how the colours in this picture are all very cool, apart from the patch of warm torchlight. The effect of these colours is to give a very quiet

and serious mood to the painting. Turner loved to experiment with colours and was very interested in the way they can affect our feelings. When he exhibited this picture he placed it next to 'War, the Exile and the Rock Limpet' which you can also see in this room. Here the colours are bright and warm, even hot, and they create a mood of complete contrast.

Turner died in 1851, nine years after this picture was exhibited, and I think that Wilkie's death at the age of 56 – he was ten years younger than Turner – perhaps made the older man realise that his own life might soon be over. In Turner's day life was shorter, and much more hazardous for people of all ages. Disease, discomfort and natural accidents and disasters were more widespread than they are today. People were much more aware of the closeness of death, and more willing to talk about it.

[10]

Snow Storm – Steamboat off a Harbour's Mouth
1842

This is one of Turner's most famous paintings, and with it, as you will later see, goes one of the best known stories about him. At the centre of the picture a steamboat is ploughing through heavy seas with its bow well down into a large wave on the right. Brown smoke belches out of its chimney toward the top where it is lost in the dark clouds and driving snow. The little flag on its slender mast stands bravely against the one patch of light which has defied the blackness. Underneath, the waves swirl backwards and forwards, and on the left they seem to shoot up into the sky to join the clouds and the snow. Behind the paddle-steamer to the left is a mark which looks as though it might well be another steamship caught up in this fearful storm.

This picture was painted in the same year as 'Peace: Burial at Sea' (*Illustration 9*). It is one of Turner's last works and he has used the subject of one of his earliest works (*Illustration 1*, 'The Shipwreck'). Here the swirling eye, or vortex, of the storm takes up the whole of the picture. There are no people to be seen, but if I give you Turner's full title you can see they are not left out of it altogether. He called it 'Snow Storm: Steam Boat off a Harbour's Mouth making Signals in Shallow Water, and going by the Lead. The Author was in the Storm on the Night the *Ariel* left Harwich.' In other words, Turner is telling us that he, 'the Author', was on the boat and in the storm. When a ship goes 'by the lead' a sailor uses a lead weight on the end of a rope to check the depth in shallow water.

The art critics hated the painting when it was exhibited at the Royal Academy. One of them wrote: 'This gentleman has, on former occasions, chosen to paint with cream, or chocolate, yolk of egg, or currant jelly, –

here he uses his whole array of kitchen stuff. Where the steamboat is, – where the harbour begins, or where it ends, – which are the signals, and which the author in the Ariel . . . are matters past our finding out'. Turner was hurt by the harsh words of the critics and we are told that he sat by the fire one evening, muttering to himself, 'I wonder what they think the sea's like? I wish they had been in it.'

Was Turner on the boat? He claimed he was, and although we cannot be certain, we do know that even at the age of 67, he had a remarkable thirst for experience of this kind. His explanation was this: 'I did not paint it to be understood, but I wished to show what such a scene was like; I got the sailors to lash me to the mast to observe it; I was lashed for four hours and I did not expect to escape, but I felt bound to record it if I did. But no one had any business to like the picture.'

It does not worry me if the story is literally true or not. Turner makes me see things I have not seen before, and he also makes me experience the storm in my imagination. I agree it is not a likeable experience, but it is very exciting in a terrifying way. It is one of those rare moments when art and real life come together, and it is impossible to say where either begins or ends.

Joseph Mallord William Turner, 'Self-Portrait', *Tate Gallery*

Turner

PERSONALITY AND CHARACTER

What was Turner like? He was rather short, and as a young man he was slim and a bit of a dandy, but in middle age he became stout and very careless in the way he dressed. He was always shy and awkward in company, and could be rude and sharp. He was not a great talker, but basically I think he did like people and there are plenty of stories which show him as good-humoured if you found him in the right mood, or knew how to handle him. He particularly liked children and young people and he probably felt most at ease in their company. There are entertaining stories of the way in which he was kind to them and made drawings to amuse them.

If Turner were alive today we would probably call him a 'loner': his rudeness was most likely his way of hiding the sensitive side to his character. He was not good with words, but was tremendously gifted with creative visual skills. He was deeply moved by the natural world and by the stirring events of modern and ancient history (*Illustration 2*). He was easily hurt by unfair or stupid criticism which failed to understand or appreciate what he was trying to do (*Illustration 10*).

He was enormously excited by life and by real events, and he lived everything to the full. He liked storms at sea (*Illustration 1*), mountains, strong sunlight, and headline-making events such as the death of Nelson, the defeat of Napoleon, the burning of the Houses of Parliament, and the invention of the railway train. Turner went out of his way to experience things for himself as often as he could. Of course he needed quieter moments as well. He read a lot, and was self-educated. He wrote long poems, parts of which were printed in the catalogues with the titles of his paintings, but they are not always easy to understand and are frankly not very good. He was passionate about all aspects of nature, including country sports such as fishing and shooting. He was particularly knowledgeable about fishing, and you can see some of his fishing rods on display in the Clore Gallery.

Turner worked on his own and did not bother to take on pupils or to train others in his way of painting. He was always experimenting with new ideas and techniques, and it was this that often made people shake their heads in disbelief. Why couldn't he be content to leave things as they were, and simply satisfy everyone with paintings they liked and knew and understood? The answer in part is that Turner always wanted to be larger than life and better and more original than anyone else (*Illustration 10*).

William Havell, 'Sandycombe Lodge'. (Turner's House at Twickenham)
Private Collection

FAMILY AND FRIENDS

Turner was born in 1775, and was christened Joseph Mallord William. He always claimed that his birthday was St George's Day, 23 April, which also happens to be Shakespeare's birthday. As he was intensely patriotic I think it is only fair to believe him, although we cannot prove it for certain.

His father was a barber in Covent Garden in London. It was a well paid profession for in those days it meant looking after the wigs of fashionable and well-to-do people, as well as cutting hair and shaving beards. Turner's father encouraged him to become a painter, and he exhibited his young son's work in his shop. When Turner became famous his father lived with him and helped run his house and prepare his materials. This was important for it was not possible to go to a shop and buy everything ready-made in tubes and packets as we can now. Painters had to learn how to prepare paints and canvases and a busy painter needed a good assistant. His mother went mad and died in the Bedlam asylum when Turner was twenty-nine and his sister died at the age of eight when Turner was still a boy.

Most of the time Turner kept himself to himself, and chose his friends with care, but he could form warm friendships with those people with whom he felt a strong bond. He had two long standing relationships with women, and was the father of at least two children. He never married and I think he also was simply too bound up with his art to have time to devote to the responsibilities of a husband and father. He was obsessed with working and travelling, and so we might say that his real marriage was to his art. Other painters found him difficult to get on with, probably because he was so hard working and competitive, (*Illustration 9*), and he sometimes behaved in a deliberately odd and eccentric way so that people would notice him.

He had a close friendship with two well-to-do families who gave him encouragement and collected his paintings. They were the family of

Walter Fawkes who lived at Farnley Hall in Yorkshire, and Lord Egremont who lived at Petworth in Sussex. He visited them regularly, and sometimes spent Christmas with them, for most of his working life (*Illustration 6*).

Petworth House, Sussex, from the Park,
National Trust Photographic Library/Tim Stevens

FAME AND FORTUNE

Turner wanted to be successful, and famous and rich. He achieved all these things. He was the youngest person to be elected a full member of the Royal Academy at that time, which was the highest honour that any artist could aspire to. His work soon attracted a wide range of admirers and collectors and he was able to sell them for high prices from early on in his career (*Illustration 1*). He made sure that his work became widely known through exhibitions, and he had many commissions to make illustrations which were reproduced in books as black-and-white prints. This was one of the best ways of getting your name before the public and so becoming known even to those who did not or could not buy paintings. Many painters today make illustrations and books for the same reason.

Turner worked hard for his success. He produced a vast amount of work – over 400 oil paintings and tens of thousands of watercolours and drawings. Few artists have produced as much work as this. He also worked hard for the Royal Academy, sitting on committees, teaching students and giving lectures (although he was a very bad mumbling lecturer). This was important as the Royal Academy was the leading art institution of the day. He was also a good businessman, investing his earnings and buying property. He built a gallery in his own house in London in which he could show his paintings.

Turner realised that to make a name for himself early on he would have to give the public and collectors the types of pictures that they wanted, and he was prepared to do this. Also, he gave these pictures a new and fresh look, so he worked out an ideal combination of the old and the new (*Illustration 3*). It was only when his reputation was established beyond doubt that he began to do the work which many people could not understand (*Illustration 10*).

Turner gave a lot of thought to what would happen to his fortune and his pictures. After he became successful he kept many of his best pictures and even bought others back which he had sold earlier in his career. He was seventy-six when he died and in his will he asked that some of his oil paintings should go to the National Gallery in London so that people could study them, remember him, and see his work in the company of the greatest artists of the past. He wanted his other pictures to be sold and the money raised to be added to the rest of his fortune to form a charity to help artists who were poor and unsuccessful. His relatives were left nothing, and they went to the courts to challenge the will. There was an agreement by which the relatives were given the money and the nation was given all the pictures. In the end we are lucky to have most of Turner's works on display in one place, but surprising as it may seem, it was not precisely what Turner intended.

George Jones, 'Turner's Coffin in his Gallery at Queen Anne Street', *Ashmolean Museum, Oxford*

TRAVELS

Each year Turner spent a lot of time travelling at home or abroad. At home he went from the north coast of Scotland to the south coast of England, and from East Anglia to Wales. In Europe the countries that most interested him were Italy, Switzerland, Germany and France (*Illustrations 7 and 8*). Travelling became much easier during Turner's lifetime, but even so there were many difficulties. The wars in Europe which lasted until Napoleon was defeated at Waterloo in 1815, frequently made journeys there impossible. Roads were bad, carriages were small, without springs, and gave a very bumpy ride. Ships were slow and uncomfortable. In winter a traveller would freeze with cold and in summer nearly expire with the heat. There were none of the fast, easy and air conditioned facilities that we have today. However, Turner was never put off and until the end of his life he never ceased to travel. In fact, I think he was rather stimulated by the discomforts and the disasters, because they were another reminder of how overpowering the forces of nature can be.

He travelled for a number of reasons. He loved to see new places. Britain has magnificent scenery, but foreign places enabled him to see sights that could not be experienced at home. There were the massive mountains of Switzerland, the picturesque river valleys and castles of Germany, and the warm golden light of Italy which is totally different to the cool grey light of England (*Illustrations 4 and 5*). Turner was always searching for new experiences in front of nature. Travel also enabled him to see works of art at first hand in foreign collections, and this too was an important experience. He knew he could learn much from the great artists of the past, and I think he liked the idea that he was standing in the places and seeing the sights that they had seen.

LANDSCAPES AND SEASCAPES

Nearly all Turner's pictures are landscapes and seascapes. When he does include people, or uses them to act out a story, they usually play second string to landscape and nature which was his real love.

He was excited by nature in all her moods. His greatest passion was for the destructive forces of nature. He loved fierce storms, dark skies, avalanches and shipwrecks (*Illustration 1*). But he also loved the kinder side of nature. Many of his paintings show fresh and delicate sunlight, cool breezes, calm sunsets or those sweet and tranquil moments which we so often fail to notice (*Illustration 4*). His genius was to see all these different qualities clearly, feel them deeply and to know how to turn his deep feelings into memorable pictures.

When Turner started his career people did not think that painting landscapes and seascapes was a very ambitious aim for an artist. Painters who wanted to be taken seriously made pictures from the great stories of Greek and Roman mythology or from the Bible. Even portrait painting was considered better than landscape. One of Turner's major achievements was to show that landscapes and seascapes should be taken seriously. He studied the sort of pictures that everyone admired, and showed that he could paint just as well (*Illustration 3*).

Turner's early landscapes and seascapes were based on a careful study of the Old Masters of the Italian and Dutch Schools of the sixteenth and seventeenth centuries, and he continued to be influenced by them throughout his life (*Illustrations 5 and 7*). However his art began to change dramatically after he went to Italy for the first time in 1819. The heat, light and strong colours overwhelmed him. He found a new face of nature, quite different to that of Northern Europe, and soon his paintings became much more romantic and personal (*Illustrations 5 and 8*). The sun became an obsession and he came to look on it in a mystical and almost religious way. When he died it is said that his last words were, 'The sun is God.'

WORKING METHODS

Some artists are skilled in several art forms. For example, the great Italian sculptor Michelangelo was also a painter and architect. Some artists design for the stage or cinema, or turn their hand to making or decorating pottery. But Turner was exclusively a painter.

His major exhibition pictures were painted in oil paints as this was the only suitable material in general use for large-scale paintings. In his early works he uses smooth paint which he usually applied in the traditional old master technique of transparent glazes, rather like layers of clear varnish (*Illustration 3*). But as we know, Turner was always experimenting, and in his later work you will be able to see how the paint gets thicker and rougher. Sometimes he put it straight onto the canvas, with a knife rather

S.W. Parrott, 'Turner on Varnishing Day', *The Ruskin Gallery, Collection of the Guild of St. George, Sheffield*

than a brush, and sometimes I suspect he used his fingers. This rough and very direct technique can look quite up-to-date and exciting to our eyes, but to people in Turner's own day it was often shocking and considered simply bad painting (*Illustration 10*).

The big oil paintings were usually produced in Turner's studio in London, but many preliminary sketches and studies had often been made, and much looking and planning had taken place (*Illustration 6*). On his travels he would have stuffed in his pockets small notebooks in which he made endless pencil sketches of things that he had seen. In the evenings he might well sit alone making free-flowing watercolours of things he wanted to remember, such as a special light effect in the sky, and these would be used to develop a big exhibition picture (*Illustrations 2* and *8*). We need to remember that he did not have the handy portable equipment and paint in tubes that we have, so that oil painting out of doors was not very practicable. You can see some of the basic materials from which Turner made up his paints on display in the Clore Gallery.

Some of Turner's watercolours are very finely detailed; these were made for sale or for engravers to copy for illustrated books. Other watercolours are only a few washes of colour, and these were probably made as experiments or as quick notes to record a memory (*Illustration 8*). There are descriptions of Turner saturating the paper with water, scrabbling, scratching, and making a chaotic mess, which eventually, as if by magic, became a glorious finished picture.

He was also fascinated by colour, and towards the end of his life studied the most up-to-date theories about colour and the way in which our moods and emotions can be influenced by different colours (*Illustration 9*). As I am sure you will have gathered, Turner was no respecter of other people's rules. He was constantly experimenting and prepared to try anything. He had a wonderful eye, a prodigious memory, and a vivid imagination. His mind was constantly full of pictures, and he was prepared to do anything to make those pictures come alive.

Turner's Palette, *Tate Gallery*

Turner's Watercolour Pouch,
Private Collection

Turner's Paint Box, *Tate Gallery*

Turner's Times

FOREIGN AFFAIRS

Turner lived through one of the most exciting periods of British and European history. For the first half of his life Britain was at war, and throughout his life he saw Britain and France gain and lose empires. In 1776, just after he was born, the American colonies declared their independence. It was an enormous blow to British prestige, and it led to war with France, Spain and Holland. Because Britain is a small island she has always depended on the Royal Navy to protect her from invasion, and on her merchant fleet to import and export goods and raw materials around the world. During the eighteenth and nineteenth centuries, and particularly during Turner's lifetime, Britain was acquiring land and territories overseas which she wanted to control and govern for reasons of trade and political influence. This often brought her into conflict with other European countries who were attempting to do the same thing. As a result of the war of 1776 Britain temporarily lost control of the seas, the first time this had happened since before the attempted invasion by the Spanish Armada in 1588. It must have seemed a terrible disaster. Fortunately the war came to an end in 1783, and although Britain regained her sea power, she lost her American colonies, being forced to give up all the land in America between the Atlantic and the Mississippi. Turner was a young boy at the time, and so would have been very conscious of these events, and much influenced by them, as we all are by our first childhood experiences. I am sure it is one of the reasons why he was so fascinated by the sea and by the rise and fall of empires, and often used them as subjects for his pictures (*Illustrations 1* and *3*).

When Turner was fourteen the French revolution exploded like a bomb in the heart of Paris. Four years later in 1793 the French royal family was sent to the guillotine, and every country in Europe felt the shock waves,

James Gillray, 'The Plumb-pudding in Danger'
Private Collection

and looked at the political events that were taking place in France with differing emotions. Some people were horrified by the extinction of the monarchy; others were optimistic that a new and fairer society would emerge. The first years of the Revolution were marked by bitter feuding and bloodshed, and in the end a new leader came to power – Napoleon. His armies soon marched across Europe, taking control of the countries they invaded and growing more and more self confident. They marched eastwards and invaded Russia, but this was a disastrous step which led to the ill-fated retreat from Moscow in the winter of 1812 (*Illustration 2*). For the British, only the Royal Navy, commanded by Nelson, stood as protection against French tyranny. The great naval victories such as Trafalgar must have seemed like miracles for the threat of invasion by Napoleon was very real. These dramatic events added yet another dimension to Turner's pictures of the sea and the rise and fall of empires.

Napoleon was finally defeated on land, by the Duke of Wellington, at the Battle of Waterloo in 1815. At the Congress of Vienna in 1816 the victorious nations shared what they had won. Britain gained new colonies overseas, and in the following years the British Empire continued to grow and British merchant ships helped to develop new economic prosperity.

Jaques Louis David, 'Napoleon Crossing the Alps', *The Bridgeman Art Library/Schloss Charlottenburg, Berlin*

Francisco de Goya, 'The Duke of Wellington', *Reproduced by Courtesy of the Trustees, The National Gallery, London*

In Europe there was a long period of peace. Foreign travel became possible again, and for the next thirty years Turner made regular visits to the Continent (*Illustration 5*).

At the very end of Turner's life Europe was rocked by political troubles. 1848 is called 'The year of Revolutions'. New political and socialist groups challenged the established Governments, and in many countries there was fighting in the streets. These revolutionary groups were partly following the example of the French Revolution half a century before, and in part fighting for social changes, for the industrial developments had produced much poverty, hardship and squalor. This time the established governments and monarchies were not overthrown, but Turner must have been aware again how war and revolution had come close to changing the British way of life which he so greatly enjoyed (*Illustration 4*).

SOCIAL CHANGES AT HOME

British society changed dramatically during Turner's lifetime. There was a massive increase in the population of Britain. When Turner was born in 1775 it numbered about 9 million. When he died in 1851 it numbered about 20 million. Away from London the change was reflected most significantly in the new manufacturing towns of the Midlands and North of England. For example the population of Birmingham increased about four times between 1775 and 1851. The census of the population which was made in 1851 showed that for the first time in our history more people lived in towns than in the country, and this came as a shock, for it showed in cold figures how great the changes had been.

This was the time when the factory system of production was developing as one aspect of the Industrial Revolution. The Yorkshire and Lancashire woollen and cotton industries were established, and they used the new coal-fired steam engines. The old cottage industries declined, and workers were driven off the land, into the new towns and sometimes into terrible slums and working conditions. The new iron industries were also developing, making bridges, furniture, buildings, machines, ships and steam engines. Understandably there was great pressure for social reform to get rid of miseries and injustice, and to create a political system that would reflect the shift in power away from the old landed aristocracy to the new industrial classes. For the nation generally it was a time of rapidly increasing prosperity, although this was not shared equally by all. Trade unions were made legal. The first Factory Acts introduced State control to the new industrial system. Slavery was abolished in 1833, and in 1832 the Great Reform Act extended the right to vote, although it was bitterly resisted by many, and there were serious riots and the threat of revolution before it became law. Two of the most influential books ever written about economics were written in Turner's lifetime although I doubt if he read either of them. Just after he was born Adam Smith published *The Wealth of*

Gustave Doré, 'Over London by Rail'
from *London, Gustave Dore and Blanchard Jerrold*, 1872

Nations, and just before he died Marx and Engels published *The Communist Manifesto*.

There were many domestic changes. The police force was created in 1829, and in 1840 Rowland Hill introduced the penny post. By 1820 most major towns were using gas light for streets, shops and public buildings. Britain had become the greatest industrial nation in the world, and this prominence was celebrated in the year of Turner's death at the Great Exhibiton of 1851. The exhibition also aimed to promote Britain as the workshop of the world, and to encourage peace and harmony through international trade. It was held in a vast glass and concrete building in Hyde Park which was called 'The Crystal Palace'. We do not know whether Turner visted it, although he was living in London at the time. Nevertheless he shared many of the qualities that built the prosperity which the exhibition celebrated. These were a belief in inventing and experimenting by trial and error, a shrewd business sense and the willingness to take risks.

THE CHANGING FACE OF BRITAIN

As we have seen, Turner was a great traveller, and the means of travel altered significantly during his lifetime. In his early days all long journeys were time-consuming and uncomfortable. London to York (about 200 miles) would have taken four days. But Turner would have seen new roads and bridges built under the influence of pioneers like MacAdam and Telford, and the turnpike system led to the great coaching days of 1820–1840 which are celebrated in many prints, in Dickens's novel *The Pickwick Papers*, and in the remaining old coaching inns. By 1836 the journey from London to York took only twenty hours and travel all over the British Isles had become much easier and more comfortable. Eventually the turnpike system was overtaken by the railways. The Liverpool to Manchester line was opened in 1830 with Stephenson's famous 'Rocket', and there were two great periods of railway building and speculation in 1835–7 and 1844–7. Thomas Cook launched his first package tour in 1841. Turner's great painting 'Rain, Steam and Speed' in the National Gallery records his excitement at this new means of transport. Nevertheless many people opposed the building of the railways, and many lost their lives in their construction.

Transport by sea was changing too. The old sailing ships were being replaced by the new coal-fired paddle steamers, and wooden hulls were giving way to iron. The first crossing of the Atlantic by sail and steam was in 1819, and by steam alone in 1838. Of the many new inventions, Turner would surely have been aware of the first successful experiments with photography by Fox-Talbot and Daguerre, and the installation of the first electric telegraph between London and Slough.

The countryside and the cities and towns were also changing. Many new industrial cities were being built in what had been rural areas, and many of the old market towns expanded and absorbed surrounding villages. Canals built extensively in the 1790s changed the face of the

Cover illustration for the Ballad *The Express Gallop*, by Charles d'Albert, *Hulton Picture Company*

landscape, but they tended to follow the contours of the land, and were less violent in the changes they brought than were the railways which cut straight through the countryside. Perhaps Turner was excited by the way these engineering works brought nature under control. At the same time the Enclosure Acts were already changing the old method of strip farming and allowing the great estates to be formed with the fields, hedges and woods that have become so typical of the English countryside. These changes encouraged the development of new methods of scientific farm-

Isambard Kingdom Brunel, *National Portrait Gallery Archive*

ing, crop rotation and animal breeding which led to an age of agricultural prosperity. As always Turner would have been alert to all of these momentous changes. They were part of his daily life. He would have read about them in newspapers, seen them with his own eyes, and discussed them with his friends. They also became part of his paintings, and we need to remember that these events and details which can seem safe and nostalgic to us, were up-to-date and challenging for the people who saw them at first hand or in Turner's pictures.

THE ROMANTIC MOVEMENT

Turner's times were prodigiously creative in all the arts. Many of our best loved musical compositions, novels, poems, and paintings were made during these years, and have remained popular and inspiring ever since. So let us focus on two questions. Who are the people who were so creative? And why were they?

Music is a good starting point. If we had lived at the same time as Turner, i.e. had been born in 1775 and died in 1851, we would have been aware of the last works of Mozart and Haydn; Beethoven, Schubert, Weber, Mendelssohn, and Chopin would all have lived and died before

Eugène Delacroix, 'Frédéric Chopin'
Bridgeman Art Library/Musée du Louvre, Paris

[70]

us; and we would have known work by Schumann, Berlioz, Liszt, Wagner and Verdi. And it is an odd fact that those who had lived and died in our lifetime all died young, mostly before they were fifty, and all before they were fifty-seven.

In literature we would have been aware that the following poets had been born after us, and died before us, again at early ages: Byron, Keats, Shelley, Coleridge. Wordsworth was the exact contemporary of Turner. We could have read all the novels of Sir Walter Scott, Jane Austen, Emily Brontë and Charlotte Brontë, and we could be reading the early novels of Dickens. If we knew French and German we could have read the novels of Victor Hugo, and Goethe. Furthermore we would have found that all the poets and writers shared our love of travel, adventure, landscape and wild scenery. Their novels and poetry are rich with adventures of childhood, unrequited love, heroes living in exile, and people fighting for liberty.

The two British painters of this period whom we commemorate today are Turner and Constable, although at the time Constable's pictures were not popular or well thought of. In Germany the most celebrated painter is Caspar David Friedrich; and in France the famous names are David, Géricault, Ingres and Delacroix; in Spain the great painter of this period is Goya. Nearly all of them overlap with Turner for most of their working lives.

I am afraid I have ended up by giving you a list of names, but what a list! You may well know some of the music or poems or paintings already, but I hope that the list will at least give you a starting point to explore, read, listen and look further; there was so much marvellous work created at this time, and how rich and stirring it often can be, Turner's included.

It is not easy to explain why there was so much creative talent, although I think we can pick out features that are common to all these artists, musicians and writers, and which can help us to understand. We call the works of this period the Romantic Movement, and all of the Romantics shared a number of common attitudes. They believed passionately in themselves as individuals. They loved new experiences. They thought the imagination should be given every freedom to explore whatever it wanted. They liked taking risks, and they lived life to the full – so they loved deeply, and often died young. Looking back at them, they appear as some of the great heroes of music, painting and writing because even in their own day they were larger than life. They wanted to be brilliant successes or total failures. Anything in the middle was of no interest whatsoever.

Perhaps the most important thing for the Romantics was their ability to let the imagination go free. I think that it is this that has ensured their popularity. If we listen to a Beethoven symphony or read a novel by Jane Austen we enter a different world, exciting and passionate, but it is a world in which our own imagination has a very important part to play. Maybe that world is more easily created by music and writing, for they exist in the mind. Paintings which show us the visible world have a more difficult job in expressing the inner depths of the human imagination. Some painters have, of course, succeeded in penetrating this inner world, and finding a way of expressing their imaginative vision. And I do know that it is because Turner can make my own imagination soar away and go free that I shall never grow tired of looking at, and discovering his paintings.